Gotta fix that step

First published in 2025 by OH
An Imprint of HEADLINE PUBLISHING GROUP LIMITED

1

Disclaimer:
This book has not been licensed, approved, sponsored, or endorsed by anyone involved in the creation, production or distribution of the *Modern Family* television series.

Cataloguing in Publication Data is available from the British Library

ISBN 978-1-03542-294-4

Compiled and written by: Saneaah Muhammad
Editorial: Saneaah Muhammad
Designed and typeset in Avenir by: Stephen Carey
Project manager: Russell Porter
Production: Marion Storz
Printed and bound in Dubai

Headline's policy is to use papers that are natural, renewable and recyclable products and made from wood grown in well-managed forests and other controlled sources. The logging and manufacturing processes are expected to conform to the environmental regulations of the country of origin.

HEADLINE PUBLISHING GROUP LIMITED
An Hachette UK Company
Carmelite House, 50 Victoria Embankment, London EC4Y 0DZ

The authorised representative in the EEA is Hachette Ireland, 8 Castlecourt Centre, Dublin 15, D15 XTP3, Ireland (email: info@hbgi.ie)

www.headline.co.uk www.hachette.co.uk

Gotta fix that step

THE LITTLE GUIDE TO MODERN FAMILY

UNOFFICIAL AND UNAUTHORIZED

CONTENTS

INTRODUCTION

Over 11 seasons, *Modern Family* didn't just make us laugh – it made us want to be part of the Dunphy-Pritchett-Tucker clan (or at least sit far enough away at Thanksgiving to avoid the drama but close enough to hear the zingers). With its mockumentary style, relatable chaos and perfectly timed one-liners, the show became a cultural phenomenon, winning 22 Emmy Awards, a Golden Globe and earning critical acclaim for redefining the modern sitcom. It was a ratings juggernaut, consistently ranking among television's most beloved comedies and drawing millions of viewers worldwide.

From Phil's *Phil's-osophies* to Gloria's fiery wisdom, Cam's theatrical meltdowns and Haley's effortless burns, *Modern Family* mastered the art of saying exactly what we were all thinking – but funnier. It gave us heartwarming moments wrapped in sarcasm, life lessons disguised as dad jokes and enough petty comebacks to last a lifetime. Whether it was Jay struggling with new-age parenting, Claire micromanaging her way through life or Mitchell sighing his way through Cam's dramatics, every character felt like someone we knew (or were).

But beyond the laughs, the show gave us something deeper – a celebration of the perfectly imperfect nature of family. It reminded us that love comes in all shapes, sizes and sarcastic remarks, and that even in the midst of chaos, there's always a reason to come together (preferably with wine, if you're Claire).

This little guide is a tribute to the best *Modern Family* quotes and facts – the moments that made us laugh and cry, and cemented the show as one of the greatest sitcoms of all time. From its sharpest comebacks to its most heartfelt wisdom, this is your ultimate companion to everything that made this show iconic – a *Modern Family-osophy*, if you will.

CHAPTER one

Peerenting, Pritchett-Style

Welcome to the wonderful world of Pritchett-parenting, where logic takes a backseat and chaos drives.

Claire's got a schedule for her schedule, Phil's got his "dad wisdom" (questionable at best) and Jay just wants a nap.

But hey, it works… *sometimes*. It's like a circus, but with less juggling and more unsolicited advice.

I'm the cool dad. That's my thing. I'm hip. I surf the Web. I text.
LOL: Laugh out loud.
OMG: Oh, my God.
WTF: Why the face?
You know, I know all the dances to *High School Musical*.

”

Phil tells us how to be a cool dad, admittedly and unknowingly getting some of the acronyms wrong.

Season 1, Episode 1: "Pilot"
"25 Hilarious *Modern Family* Quotes to Live By", readersdigest.ca

You know how growing up we all have that voice inside our head that tells us we're not good enough? Well, mine was outside my head driving me to school.

”

Claire confesses her strenuous relationship with her mother.

Season 1, Episode 4: "The Incident"
"25 Hilarious *Modern Family* Quotes to Live By", readersdigest.ca

Buddy, the three of us were having a girls' day. You get it.

Phil, to Luke, when Luke feels left out of a memory of when his two sisters spent the day with their dad.

Season 6, Episode 23: "Crying Out Loud"
getyarn.io

Sometimes things work out just the way you want. Sometimes they don't. But you have to hang in there because 90% of being a dad is just showing up.

”

Jay tells us the most significant part of being a dad: Just being there.

Season 1, Episode 2: "The Bicycle Thief"
"*Modern Family*: 13 Best Inspiring Quotes About Relationships", screenrant.com, November 16, 2021

Act like a parent, talk like a peer. I call it 'peerenting'. I learned it from my own dad who used to walk into my room and say, 'What's up, sweat hog?'

Phil gives us some friendly "peerenting" advice.

Season 1, Episode 4: "The Incident"
"The 10 Best 'Modern Family' Quotes, Ranked", collider.com, February 23, 2024

Family Exposé

In 2012, five main cast members (Ty Burrell, Julie Bowen, Sofía Vergara, Jesse Tyler Ferguson and Eric Stonestreet) sued 20th Century Fox over their salaries. Ed O'Neill, who was already making $200,000 per episode, joined them in negotiations.

The result? The adults got a pay bump to $150,000–$175,000 per episode, and the child actors' salaries jumped from $15,000 to $70,000 per episode.

Ed O'Neill took a slight pay cut to help balance the salaries for the rest of the cast – a true family on set and in real life.

That's the whole point of a surprise party: You take somebody you really love and you play 'em like a fool.

”

Jay is perhaps a little confused on how to treat those you love.

Season 4, Episode 12: "Party Crasher"
"25 Hilarious *Modern Family* Quotes to Live By", readersdigest.ca

Manny comes from a long line of fishers and smugglers. But I encourage the fishing.

”

Gloria encourages Manny to embrace his roots… though not all of them.

Season 1, Episode 16: "Fears"
"20 Unapologetic Quotes By *Modern Family*'s Gloria That Make Her TV's Feistiest Character", July 5, 2016, scoopwhoop.com

Breaking the ice with the other parents has been a little tough. Cam and I are the only white parents, the only gay parents, the only parents that find us funny.

”

Mitchell and Cam struggle to fit in with other parents... but at least they have humour to keep them going.

Season 7, Episode 11: "Spread Your Wings"
"21 Quotes We Love From *Modern Family*'s Mitchell Pritchett!", parade.com, March 6, 2021

"I've always said that if my son thinks of me as one of his idiot friends, I've succeeded as a dad."

Phil's definition of success as a father is acting like an idiot with his son.

Season 3, Episode 4: "Door to Door"
"The 20 Best Phil Dunphy Quotes", *Paste* magazine, July 21, 2012

Family On and Off the Screen

From the very start, the adult cast made a pact that none of them would submit themselves for Lead Actor awards – only Supporting Actor – so that everyone was seen as equally important.

The pact paid off, with multiple cast members receiving Emmy nominations in the Supporting Actor and Actress categories over the years. Ty Burrell (Phil), Eric Stonestreet (Cam) and Julie Bowen (Claire) took home two Emmy wins each.

This commitment to fairness behind the scenes mirrored the show's on-screen dynamic – a loving family where everyone mattered.

Jay never wants me help him with his business, and now suddenly Manny doesn't want to listen to me either. It's very frustrating. I have all the answers!

Gloria gets frustrated that no one in her family will take her advice – she can help them all!

Season 3, Episode 5: "Hit and Run"
imdb.com

It can be challenging finding playmates for an exceptional child. I don't mean to brag, but that's why I didn't have any friends.

Mitchell explains why he didn't have any friends… he was just too smart for them.

Season 6, Episode 3: "The Cold"
"37 Quotes That Make You Wish 'Modern Family' Was Your Family", puckermob.com

Look at them. A minute ago, they were babies, and now they're driving, and soon we'll all be dead.

”

Claire might be looking a little too far into the future.

Season 2, Episode 1: "The Old Wagon"
"The 10 Best 'Modern Family' Quotes, Ranked", collider.com, February 23, 2024

Don't get me wrong, the Dunphys have had some great days. We just have a little trouble stringing them together. Our record was eight consecutive blissful days – December 2007. It was our Hanukkah.

”

Claire reminisces on the great Dunphy days.

Season 6, Episode 16: "Connection Lost"
tvshowtranscripts.ourboard.org

My kids are helpless, but maybe that's okay. Because years from now when they have their own houses, they'll call me on their hologram phones and say, 'Help me, Dad. You're my only hope.' And I'll be the happiest father in sector 7. Or sector 12, if we're doing really well.

Phil stops worrying about raising his kids to be independent because he'll always be there for them.

Season 4, Episode 21: "Career Day"
modernfamily.fandom.com

If your plan is to cry in front of Lily, forget it. You're too emotionally constipated.

Claire, to Mitchell, who believes Lily doesn't have empathy because of his inability to express his emotions.

Season 6, Episode 23: "Crying Out Loud"
transcripts.foreverdreaming.org

I always wanted a daughter… to dress her up in pretty dresses, do her hair, her nails, her makeup. No one knows this, but for the first year of his life, I made up Manny like a girl and told everyone that he was my daughter. But just for a few times, I didn't want to mess with his head. When he found the pictures, I told him that it was his twin sister who died.

”

Gloria confesses how she raised Manny… a little confusingly.

Season 1, Episode 3: "Come Fly With Me"
"35+ 'Modern Family' Quotes To Make You Feel Like A Tucker-Pritchett-Dunphy", scarymommy.com, January 22, 2021

Look, everybody learns in different ways. My intellectual approach just wasn't right for Gloria, and it probably wasn't right for Lily. It's humbling to admit, but I'm just too smart to teach.

Mitchell, humble about his intelligence as always.

Season 7, Episode 12: "Clean for a Day"
"21 Quotes We Love From *Modern Family*'s Mitchell Pritchett!", parade.com, March 6, 2021

I always felt bad for people with emotionally distant fathers; it turns out I'm one of them. It's a miracle I didn't end up a stripper.

”

Phil's career turned out to be successful, despite having a father who struggled to share feelings with him... once.

Season 1, Episode 21: "Travels with Scout"
"35+ 'Modern Family' Quotes To Make You Feel Like A Tucker-Pritchett-Dunphy", scarymommy.com, January 22, 2021

Adopting Lily, marrying Mitchell, high-school football championship and sitting behind Sarah Jessica Parker at *Wicked*.

”

Cam lists the most important moments of his life… of course, SJP made the list.

Season 6, Episode 20: "Knock 'Em Down"
transcripts.foreverdreaming.org

More than anything, I want my girls to stop fighting and be close. I want them to share clothes and do each other's hair and gossip about boys, like I used to do with Mitchell.

Claire reminisces about her childhood with Mitchell… he was almost like a sister to her.

Season 2, Episode 17: "Two Monkeys and a Panda"
"35+ 'Modern Family' Quotes To Make You Feel Like A Tucker-Pritchett-Dunphy", scarymommy.com, January 22, 2021

Phil Wisdom

The role of Phil Dunphy was written specifically for Ty Burrell, but the network was hesitant about casting him. They only agreed after the producers filmed a test reel proving how perfect he was for the role.

Many of Phil's best moments were improvised by Ty, including his famous *Phil's-osophy* book. The writers just let him go wild with dad wisdom.

That's when it hit me – my daughters know nothing about home care and maintenance. I don't want them to be dependent. It's up to me to show them what a modern, self-sufficient woman looks like.

Phil shows his daughters what an independent woman looks like… as a modern dad.

Season 4, Episode 18: "The Wow Factor"
modernfamily.fandom.com

The family needs a leader, and I can't do it forever.

Jay, to Alex, when she feels overwhelmed.

Season 6, Episode 19: "Grill, Interrupted"
tvfanatic.com, April 2, 2015

Not that there's any shame in learning a trade. Air conditioners are always gonna break.

”

Claire, to Luke, encouraging him to pursue a career in the shadow of his genius older sister Alex.

Season 6, Episode 19: "Grill, Interrupted"
transcripts.foreverdreaming.org

CHAPTER two

The Dunphy Guide to Disaster

Being a Dunphy means no two days are the same. Claire's got her eyes on every detail (and occasionally on the ceiling when it all comes crashing down), while Phil's turning a home improvement project into an Olympic sport.

Add in some overachievements, teenage drama and trampolining without pants and you've got the blueprint for total family mayhem.

And they wouldn't have it any other way.

It's got all those doo-dads. I don't know what to do with those doo-dads.

”

Jay seems uninterested in the fancy new grill that Phil bought for him, much to Phil's dismay.

Season 6, Episode 19: "Grill, Interrupted"
getyarn.io

You're never alone when you have books.

”

Alex proudly prefers fictional characters over real ones.

Season 2, Episode 9: "Earthquake"
"*Modern Family*: 13 Best Inspiring Quotes About Relationships", screenrant.com, November 16, 2021

The only problem was that people kept interrupting. I didn't need a phone anymore. I just needed a quiet place to find out how they kill that mockingbird.

”

Haley longs to finish reading *How to Kill a Mockingbird*, after living without her phone for the day.

Season 9, Episode 3: "Catch of the Day"
"*Modern Family*: One Quote From Each Main Character That Goes Against Their Personality", screenrant.com, October 1, 2021

Um, well you know how in a fairy tale there's always a potion that makes the princess fall asleep and then the guys start kissing her? Well, this is like that, except you don't wake up in a castle, you wake up in a frat house with a bad reputation.

Phil's answer to Alex's question: "What's Jägermeister?"

Season 1, Episode 14: "Moon Landing"
"37 Quotes That Make You Wish 'Modern Family' Was Your Family", puckermob.com

Gotta fix that step!

Phil, throughout the entire show, as he consistently trips on a broken step on the staircase in the Dunphy home.

"The Top 10 Phil Dunphy Quotes on 'Modern Family'", ontapsportsnet.com, April 4, 2024

The Staircase Gag

In Season 1, Ty Burrell (Phil Dunphy) accidentally tripped on the Dunphy staircase while filming a scene.

The writers loved it so much that they made it a running joke, with Phil constantly saying, "Gotta fix that step."

Funny. I always thought I'd be found dead in a bird suit at the bottom of the Grand Canyon.

”

Luke despairs over dying from a deadly worm that Gloria pretended was in a bottle of alcohol he and Manny drank (even though she secretly switched it with water) rather than the death he wanted – to which Manny responds, "You still will, buddy."

Season 6, Episode 19: "Grill, Interrupted"
imdb.com

A ladybug landed on me today. How could this happen?

”

Phil starts panicking when his dream of creating "Dunphy Tower" goes awry.

Season 8, Episode 14: "Heavy is the Head"
modernfamily.fandom.com

Manny: Do you realize that in two years we'll be graduating?

Luke: Quiet, Manny. I think I'm moving the ball with my mind.

Manny: Well, I'll be graduating.

Manny thinks ahead to his cap and gown while Luke focuses on his self-proclaimed special powers.

Season 2, Episode 22: "Good Cop Bad Dog"
modernfamily.fandom.com

Today I get to talk about the love of my life. Residential real estate.

”

Phil, the husband and father, talks about what he loves the most… his job.

Season 4, Episode 21: "Career Day"
"11 of the Funniest Real Estate Quotes (and Advice) from *Modern Family's* Phil Dunphy", labcoatagents.com, July 20, 2020

Quick, girls. Famous Danny from *Moonstruck*. Aiello!

”

Phil can never answer the phone with a simple hello.

Season 3, Episode 15: "Aunt Mommy"
modernfamily.fandom.com

Phil's Phone-isms

These are some of the best ways Phil answers the phone throughout the show:

"Nature's sure-fire sunburn remedy? Aloe!"

"What instrument does Yo-Yo Ma play? Cello!"

"Who sang 'Evil Woman'? ELO!"

"What's my favourite hospital food? Jell-o!"

"What's the most dangerous type of uranium cake? Yellow!"

"What nickname did Jennifer Lopez steal from Jon Lovitz? J-Lo!"

"What's the best first-person shooter about genetically modified space marines? Halo!"

"Phil, where were nationals Senior Year? Cleveland, Oh ... Hi-o!"

"What's the ring around an angel's head? Halo!"

The bonerface! You win that award, everyone called you 'bonerface'.

Luke wins the least-wanted award (The Boniface Award) after Claire nudges him to the top of the list.

Season 6, Episode 21: "Integrity"
transcripts.foreverdreaming.org

You want to get ahead? Don't play by the rules. Turns out nice guys finish last in this cold dog-eat-dog world.

”

Phil learns that being the nice guy doesn't always work out so well.

Season 3, Episode 18: "Send Out the Clowns"
modernfamily.fandom.com

Look, I have no problem drinking. I can literally do it standing on my head. But A, not with my parents. Plus, also I needed to stay sharp because they were obviously up to something and I was in no mood. I barely got 10 hours of sleep last night.

”

Haley struggles to stay alert as her parents suspiciously invite her to go drinking.

Season 5, Episode 13: "Three Dinners"
"*Modern Family:* Best Haley Dunphy Quotes", screenrant.com, May 9, 2019

It's called growing up and having my own interests, just like the preacher's daughter in your precious *Footloose*.

99

Luke uses Phil's favourite movie against him, cutting smoother than Kevin Bacon's dance moves.

Season 5, Episode 11: "And One to Grow On"
modernfamily.fandom.com

Phil's tinkling with the new grill, so you better collect some old photographs for the memorial.

”

Jay expresses concern for Phil's well-being in his usual undermining tone… reserved solely for Phil.

Season 6, Episode 19: "Grill, Interrupted"
transcripts.foreverdreaming.org

I am brave. Roller coasters? Love 'em. Scary movies? I've seen *Ghostbusters* like, seven times. I regularly drive through neighbourhoods that have only recently been gentrified. So yeah, I'm pretty much not afraid of anything… except for clowns.

Phil confesses his one single fear.

Season 1, Episode 9: "Fizbo"
"25 Hilarious *Modern Family* Quotes to Live By", readersdigest.ca

I've been lonely. Having a mirror in my room will be like having company.

”

Haley brings another meaning to loving your own company.

Season 5, Episode 15: "The Feud"
"35+ 'Modern Family' Quotes To Make You Feel Like A Tucker-Pritchett-Dunphy", scarymommy.com, January 22, 2021

Two things I bring to every open house? My lucky pen and a smile. I haven't sold a house all month. Do you see me saying, 'I'm done'? Never. Because there is no 'done' in 'Dunphy'.

Phil seems to be a little confused over his own last name, but we get the sentiment.

Season 5, Episode 9: "The Big Game"
"11 of the Funniest Real Estate Quotes (and Advice) from *Modern Family*'s Phil Dunphy", labcoatagents.com, July 20, 2020

Let me work my magic. It's all about creative editing. Just give me two hours… then another hour. Someone get me a chocolate milk. With extra salt.

”

Luke requires special conditions to focus on his task.

Season 2, Episode 24: "The One That Got Away"
modernfamily.fandom.com

Child Genius

In real life, Nolan Gould (Luke Dunphy) is nothing like his character.

He graduated high school at 13, has an IQ of 150 and is a longtime Mensa member (since age 4!).

He also plays multiple instruments, including the double bass, banjo, sitar, mandolin and theremin.

Check the structural integrity of the trophy case, bitches, 'cause mama's bringing home some hardware.

”

Alex celebrates the one day of the year she has some "real swagger" – Awards Day.

Season 6, Episode 21: "Integrity"
imdb.com

Alex is teaching herself Chinese, so she'll be useful when they finish buying us.

”

Phil brings Claire up to speed on what their kids are up to.

Season 3, Episode 21: "Planes, Trains and Cars"
"The 20 Best Phil Dunphy Quotes", *Paste* magazine, July 21, 2012

I am Phil Dunphy, and I am not a pervert. I, like a lot of men in this town, enjoy making love to my wife. I mean, uh… I mean with their wives. Not me, them! Look, I should probably just sit down and say nothing, but it's too late. I am standing, and I'm obviously talking, and now you're looking at me, and I feel the need to keep going.

”

Phil attempts to calm a worked-up crowd… but confusing them even more.

Season 3, Episode 13: "Little Bo Bleep"
modernfamily.fandom.com

I've been thinking of moving out for some time now. There's a line of ants going to a trick-or-treat bag in my closet, and I don't want to still be here when they get sick of candy.

”

Luke moves upstairs to the attic before he gets eaten alive by ants.

Season 3, Episode 21: "When Good Kids Go Bad"
"35+ 'Modern Family' Quotes To Make You Feel Like A Tucker-Pritchett-Dunphy", scarymommy.com, January 22, 2021

Um, things I want: robot dog, night-vision goggles, bug vacuum, GPS watch, speakers that look like rocks… I love my wife, but she sucks at giving gifts. I'm sorry for the pay-channel language, but – oh! Yogurt maker! I can't *not* think of things I want.

Phil lists the things he would love to receive.

Season 1, Episode 8: "Great Expectations"
"37 Quotes That Make You Wish 'Modern Family' Was Your Family", puckermob.com

Yes, I'm a huge dork for celebrating my 21st with my family, but my mom was crazy excited to go to a bar with me… or just go to a bar.

Haley celebrates being able to legally drink by going wild… a night out with her mother.

Season 6, Episode 10: "Haley's 21st Birthday"
"37 Quotes That Make You Wish 'Modern Family' Was Your Family", puckermob.com

I ran six miles the morning you were born, you came out of the womb ready for this!

Claire motivates Alex before a school race that will determine her position as valedictorian.

Season 6, Episode 22: "Patriot Games"
transcripts.foreverdreaming.org

Off to a Good Start

Modern Family premiered in 2009 and won two Primetime Emmys for its pilot episode, setting the stage for its massive success.

The pilot episode ended up being ABC's highest-testing comedy pilot in years, which led to an almost immediate series order.

Everything I touch turns to detention.

”

Haley despairs over her remarkable ability to get into trouble.

Season 3, Episode 3: "Phil on Wire"
"100 Best Quotes from *Modern Family*", sarahscoop.com, August 22, 2022

Happy Valenbirthaversary!

”

Phil attempts to figure out why Claire is mad… by celebrating every holiday in one.

Season 2, Episode 16: "Regrets Only"
"The Top 10 Phil Dunphy Quotes on 'Modern Family'", ontapsportsnet.com, April 4, 2024

Today is 'Ditch Day'? No way you're missing 'Ditch Day'. It's like the best week of Senior Year… day.

”

Haley, to Alex, when Alex decides not to take part in "Ditch Day".

Season 6, Episode 23: "Crying Out Loud"
transcripts.foreverdreaming.org

Thanks to 35 dollars on the Internet you are looking at the Good Reverend Philip Humphrey Dunphy.

”

Phil gets ordained online so that he can perform the ceremony at Cam and Mitchell's wedding… which they didn't exactly agree to.

Season 5, Episode 24: "The Wedding (Part 2)"
"37 Quotes That Make You Wish 'Modern Family' Was Your Family", puckermob.com

Let me meet this playa. Phil Dunphy, yo.

”

Phil attempts to intimidate Haley's new boyfriend by acting "hip"... right before he slips in baby oil and injures his back.

Season 1, Episode 1: "Pilot"
getyarn.io

Claire, you're a hard one to figure out. You don't trust bad boys, and yet you married one.

Phil reminds Claire of the bad boy she never knew she married… and still doesn't know exists.

Season 5, Episode 14: "iSpy"
"The Top 10 Phil Dunphy Quotes on 'Modern Family'", ontapsportsnet.com, April 4, 2024

I'm so stressed. I wish it was the 50s when it was healthy to drink and smoke when you're pregnant.

”

Haley longs for the days when bad decisions were simply doctors' recommendations.

Season 10, Episode 9: "Putting Down Roots"
"100 Best Quotes from *Modern Family*", sarahscoop.com, August 22, 2022

What a world it could be if people would just hate more.

Phil shares some of his (un)usual positivity.

Season 6, Episode 20: "Knock 'Em Dead"
getyarn.io

CHAPTER three

Closet? You'll Love It!

Jay's closet business is booming (we mean, as booming as closets can be), while Gloria's hot sauce empire is more like a hot mess, Manny's living in a world of poetry, melodrama and occasional pouts about his "artistic soul" and little Joe has some unusual hobbies.

Not to mention, Phil's real estate obsession has him seeing potential homes, towers and car parks everywhere. It's a family of business, creativity and regular chaos… with a whole lot of Colombian sass!

In my country, it is considered very very bad luck when your house burns down.

Gloria's roots have some unusual beliefs, or some very usual ones.

Season 3, Episode 8: "After the Fire"
"100 Best Quotes from *Modern Family*", sarahscoop.com, August 22, 2022

I've always felt out of place at public school. Like a lone petunia in an onion patch.

Manny romantizes his uniqueness – he never quite fit in with everyone else.

Season 4, Episode 19: "The Future Dunphys"
"*Modern Family*: Manny's 10 Wisest Quotes Proving He's Way Beyond His Years", screenrant.com, February 25, 2020

Closet? You'll love it!

”

Jay's famous slogan for his company, Pritchett's Closets – no one can figure out what it actually means.

Season 6, Episode 17: "Closet? You'll Love It!"
modernfamily.fandom.com

I knew we should have poured that Tequila in your bellybutton. That's why they have these systems in place.

”

Manny, to Luke, when they are fooled into believing that the fake Tequila they drank (Gloria switched it with water) contained a deadly worm.

Season 6, Episode 19: "Grill, Interrupted"
tvfanatic.com

Hey, Luke. Quick lesson. This is a coaster, it prevents rings. Thanks to you and your Dr. Pepper, my teak end table upstairs looks like the Olympic flag. Think, Luke.

Manny scolds Luke on his lack of table manners.

Season 6, Episode 19: "Grill, Interrupted"
transcripts.foreverdreaming.org

I'm Colombian. I know a fake crime scene when I see one.

”

Gloria knows a little too much about illegal activity.

Season 1, Episode 17: "Truth Be Told"
tvgag.com

Aren't we all just fragile eggs hiding behind bubble wrap and bravado?

”

Manny Delgado

Season 3, Episode 12: "Egg Drop"
"*Modern Family*: Manny's 10 Wisest Quotes Proving He's Way Beyond His Years", screenrant.com, February 25, 2020

That's it? Two questions? And I have a cheat flag? That's all it takes?

Gloria, after passing her US citizenship test a little too easily.

Season 6, Episode 22: "Patriot Games"
getyarn.io

We have a name at the office for when a deal goes south. Commission: Impossible. Maybe for some people.

Phil takes on the challenge of making the impossible possible and becoming the best realtor in Southern California.

Season 3, Episode 15: "Aunt Mommy"
modernfamily.fandom.com

Buddy, don't close yourself off from new things. I ever tell you the story about me and crab cakes? Thought I didn't like them, tried them, loved them.

Jay encourages Manny to eat his scrambled (instead of boiled) eggs with a not-so-riveting anecdote – Manny responds: "Wow. Are the movie rights available for that one?"

Season 2, Episode 18: "Boys' Night"
"6 'Modern Family' Quotes That Apply To Your Swim Family", *Swimming World* magazine, May 26, 2016

Staying up all night, it's in your blood. You come from the land of coffee and cocaine.

Mitchell reminds Gloria of her roots in an attempt to stay awake to make it to the club.

Season 6, Episode 20: "Knock 'Em Down"
tvgag.com

Child Prodigy

At age 4, Aubrey Anderson-Emmons (the actress who plays Lily Tucker-Pritchett) became the youngest person ever to receive the Screen Actors Guild Award in 2011.

The award was presented to the entire cast for Outstanding Performance by an Ensemble in a Comedy Series.

Wake up, Delgado. Black box? From Colombia? No more questions? It's obviously a human head.

Luke, to Manny, about a box belonging to Gloria. Luke then opens a box, only for Manny to shout, "Oh, my God! It's a head!"

Season 4, Episode 6: "Yard Sale"
modernfamily.fandom.com

You know what they say: House guests start to stink after three days like dead bodies.

Gloria finds a fun little twist on the phrase "Guests, like fish, begin to smell after three days."

Season 5, Episode 10: "The Old Man & the Tree"
"20 Unapologetic Quotes By *Modern Family*'s Gloria That Make Her TV's Feistiest Character", July 5, 2016, scoopwhoop.com

I saw Manny take shampoos from the hotel, so I took some things, too. Then some bigger things. I like stealing, it makes my heart go fast.

Joe's cuteness might help him get away with bad habits for now – at the end of the episode, he announces to the family, "I steal now."

Season 8, Episode 1: "A Tale of Three Cities"
modernfamily.fandom.com

When you're married to me, you're going to be yelled at many times.

”

Gloria reminds Jay of the woman he married.

Season 4, Episode 4: "The Butler's Escape"
"100 Best Quotes from *Modern Family*", sarahscoop.com, August 22, 2022

If Mom isn't a citizen when Jay 'moves on to a better place' we could be looking at a pretty hefty estate tax. I don't want to sound insensitive, but I've acquired a real taste for truffles.

Manny encourages Gloria to become a US citizen... for his own benefit.

Season 6, Episode 22: "Patriot Games"
transcripts.foreverdreaming.org

What could be more natural than your mother's tongue in your ear?

”

Gloria encourages Manny to learn Spanish rather than French… in a weird way.

Season 6, Episode 7: "Queer Eyes, Full Hearts"
"20 Unapologetic Quotes By *Modern Family's* Gloria That Make Her TV's Feistiest Character", July 5, 2016, scoopwhoop.com

I caught one of my so-called friends hitting on her. And now she's like the fetal pig we once so happily shared. Cold, unresponsive, heartless.

”

Manny despairs over losing the interest of the girl he liked.

Season 6, Episode 21: "Integrity"
transcripts.foreverdreaming.org

Comfort is not everything. My toes have been numb since my Quinceañera.

”

Gloria understands that beauty can be pain.

Season 6, Episode 1: "The Long Honeymoon"
"35+ 'Modern Family' Quotes To Make You Feel Like A Tucker-Pritchett-Dunphy", scarymommy.com, January 22, 2021

When Phil told me about this house, I offered to help. Now that Manny's away at college and Joe goes to kindergarten, I have time for one of my old hobbies – confronting the devil in all his forms.

Gloria helps Phil to cleanse a house of so-called evil spirits… or discover a wall filled with bees.

Season 9, Episode 10: "No Small Feet"
modernfamily.fandom.com

By the power vested in me by the Commercial Zoning Board, I do hereby officially break ground on the future home of Dunphy Tower… oh, that's strong soil.

”

Phil, breaking ground on the land he and Jay bought to build his dream project: Dunphy Tower – due to construction issues, the project changed from a building to a car park.

Season 8, Episode 14: "Heavy IS the Head"
transcripts.foreverdreaming.org

I gave her my heart, she gave me a picture of me as an old-time sheriff. Today was my second chance, but I couldn't even get up the nerve to say 'Hi'. Eleven-year-old Manny would be disgusted by me.

99

Manny gets to relive an old experience with a girl he liked… only to lose courage again.

Season 11, Episode 11: "Legacy"
modernfamily.fandom.com

I thought one of the advantages of marrying an older guy would be that I would get to relax. But with the swimming and running and rowing… it's how some of my relatives came to this country.

”

Gloria gets tired of Jay exercising, when all she wants to do is relax.

Season 1, Episode 23: "Hawaii"
modernfamily.fandom.com

Gloria and I are from different generations. And I won't lie: it isn't always easy. I mean, last week she thought Simon and Garfunkel were my lawyers.

99

Jay can feel the age gap between him and Gloria, and sometimes it makes for terrible jokes.

Season 1, Episode 15: "My Funky Valentine"
modernfamily.fandom.com

Everybody Gets a Birthday!

Despite the show's large cast, every main character has had a birthday scene at some point to make everyone feel included – yet another way in which the cast were a family both on and off the screen.

I bite my tongue, because in this family, they think that I am a Colombian hot head, which is crazy because a Colombian hot head is when you set somebody's head on fire. It smells terrible, but it sends a message.

”

Gloria clears up the true meaning of "hot head".

Season 6, Episode 21: "Integrity"
imdb.com

I'm dead set against drugs. 'Just Say No!' and all that stuff. But I thought, just this once for Gloria. And if I was gonna make a complete ass of myself, I didn't wanna remember it.

Jay, proving he'll do anything for his wife, including taking a pill, which he believes to be a party drug but actually turns out to be a "baby aspirin, orange-flavoured."

Season 3, Episode 7: "Treehouse"
"21 Quotes We Love From *Modern Family*'s Mitchell Pritchett!", parade.com, March 6, 2021

Manny: I know what all of you are thinking: my jacket is wrinkled. I would have ironed it, but someone here thought it would be a great idea to use the iron to make a grilled cheese sandwich.

Luke: I had bread. I had cheese. I had an iron. What was I supposed to do?

Manny tires of **Luke** getting in the way of his pristine reputation.

Season 1, Episode 23: "Hawaii"
modernfamily.fandom.com

That doesn't make any sense! Who wants to live in a world where dogs eat each other? Doggy-dog world is a beautiful world filled with little puppies.

Gloria can't understand why people use the phrase "dog-eat-dog world".

Season 2, Episode 6: "Halloween"
"20 Unapologetic Quotes By *Modern Family's* Gloria That Make Her TV's Feistiest Character", July 5, 2016, scoopwhoop.com

So, is that a birthday present for you, or an extremely late mid-life crisis?

”

Manny, to Jay, when he brings home a brand-new sports car (on loan).

Season 6, Episode 19: "Grill, Interrupted"
tvshowtranscripts.ourboard.org

Gloria makes this Colombian dish I loved when we were first dating… I lied about a lot of things back then.

Jay confesses that he doesn't always enjoy Gloria's cooking.

Season 7, Episode 15: "I Don't Know How She Does It"
modernfamily.fandom.com

I'm gonna teach him the real version, not the Colombian version. We use the pieces to play the game, not smuggle stuff out of the country.

Jay, on teaching Manny how to play chess, without realizing that Manny is already a great chess player.

Season 1, Episode 19: "Game Changer"
imdb.com

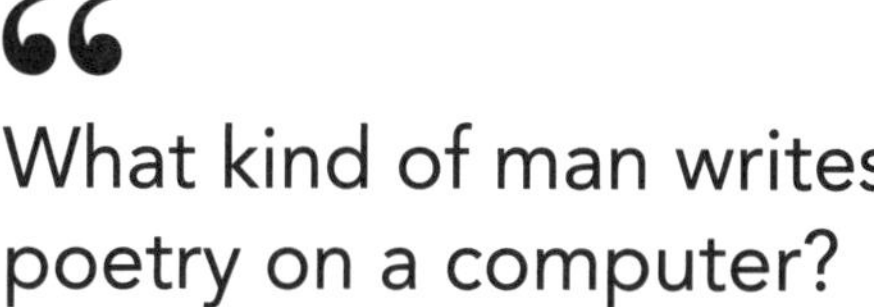

What kind of man writes poetry on a computer?

Manny reminds the world of what a true poet looks like.

Season 4, Episode 23: "Games People Play"
tvfanatic.com

So what? He's the worst person I have ever met. And there was a man in my village named 'Fabio the baby puncher'.

Gloria reminds the family of the unusual people from her past.

Season 6, Episode 21: "Integrity"
transcripts.foreverdreaming.org

If this so-called Santa Claus doesn't bring me a burgundy dinner jacket, I'm going to have a big problem.

Manny Delgado

Season 1, Episode 10: "Undeck the Halls"
tvfanatic.com

CHAPTER four

Love, Bickering and Broadway Gays

The Tucker-Pritchett household comes with show tunes, expertly timed sarcasm and just a dash of unnecessary drama (mostly from Cam – okay, entirely from Cam).

Whether they're parenting Lily, bickering over the right way to load a dishwasher or navigating Cam's latest theatrical meltdown, Mitch and Cam prove that love isn't just about compromise – it's about flair, family, and knowing when to cue the music.

OK, everybody's looking at us. I haven't been judged by this many people since I forgot my canvas bags at Whole Foods.

”

Mitchell worries about being judged for keeping Lily on a "child safety tether".

Season 3, Episode 22: "Disneyland"
"21 Quotes We Love From *Modern Family*'s Mitchell Pritchett!", parade.com, March 6, 2021

Lily, stop. You are an exotic Vietnamese beauty, Scarlett Johansson would play you in a movie, until Twitter told her she couldn't.

”

Cam reminds Lily of her beauty, while keeping up with the times.

Season 11, Episode 3: "Perfect Pairs"
modernfamily.fandom.com

Figure skaters. Oh, for god's sakes, I'll tell the story. Yes, my sister and I were actually a very good team. We were called 'Fire and Nice'. I was 'fire' 'cause of the red hair, and Claire was 'nice' because it was ironic and she wasn't.

”

Mitchell tells the story of his and Claire's short-lived figure-skating career.

Season 1, Episode 7: "En Garde"
"21 Quotes We Love From *Modern Family's* Mitchell Pritchett!", parade.com, March 6, 2021

Prepare to feel like an old denim vest because I'm about to be dazzling you.

Cam expresses his usual flair for dramatics.

Season 5, Episode 2: "First Days"
"35+ 'Modern Family' Quotes To Make You Feel Like A Tucker-Pritchett-Dunphy", scarymommy.com, January 22, 2021

Straight people always take our best stuff. First, they came for our brunches, and I said nothing.

Mitchell wants to gatekeep all his favourite hobbies.

Season 11, Episode 5: "The Last Halloween"
"21 Quotes We Love From *Modern Family's* Mitchell Pritchett!", parade.com, March 6, 2021

That's offensive. There're all kinds of gays. You've got your Broadway gays, your gym gays, your twinks, your bears, your otters, your 'Hey Girl!' gays. You've got your pups, your cubs, your chubs, and most prominently, you've got your average-Joes-who-you-would-never-know-are-gay gays.

Cam, to Jay, when he groups gay people into the same category.

Season 6, Episode 20: "Knock 'Em Down"
getyarn.io

I can't go to jail. I'm a gay prosecutor, there's no prison gangs for that!

Mitchell worries about not fitting in all over again.

Season 11, Episode 18: Finale: Part 2
"100 Best Quotes from *Modern Family*", sarahscoop.com, August 22, 2022

Really, Mitchell? The worst Halloween ever? You had squeaky thighs; I lost a childhood.

Cam recalls a painful childhood Halloween memory of when he was framed for taking all the Halloween candies out of the bowl.

Season 2, Episode 6: "Halloween"
"17 Comebacks From Cameron Tucker From 'Modern Family' That Made Me Go 'SLAYYY'", buzzfeed.com, June 8, 2022

Everyone has their strengths. I'm a great gift-giver.

Mitchell proudly reveals his slightly unusual strengths.

Season 7, Episode 1: "Summer Lovin"
"21 Quotes We Love From *Modern Family*'s Mitchell Pritchett!", parade.com, March 6, 2021

“I’m sort of like Costco. I’m big, I’m not fancy and I dare you to not like me.”

Cam shows himself a little self-love.

Season 3, Episode 1: "Come Fly With Me"
"35+ 'Modern Family' Quotes To Make You Feel Like A Tucker-Pritchett-Dunphy", scarymommy.com, January 22, 2021

So, my interest in football ended as suddenly and dramatically as the climax of *West Side Story*. I'm a musical-theater fan.

”

Mitchell proves that his interests lie with the creative arts… not so much with sports.

Season 1, Episode 5: "Coal Digger"
"21 Quotes We Love From *Modern Family*'s Mitchell Pritchett!", parade.com, March 6, 2021

Ya' know, my parents never talked to me about anything sexual. They just sent me to the stables when the horses were breeding and wow did that create some unreasonable expectations.

”

Cam reveals that he had a wildly different experience to "the talk".

Season 10, Episode 12: "Blasts From the Past"
"100 Best Quotes from *Modern Family*", sarahscoop.com, August 22, 2022

All Inclusive

Modern Family wasn't just a hit comedy – it was also recognized for its impact on LGBTQ+ representation.

The show won a GLSEN Respect Award for portraying positive and diverse storylines.

I came out of the closet in my mid-twenties. I had to actually come out to my dad three times before he finally acknowledged it. I'm not sure if maybe he was hoping he heard it wrong, like I had said, 'Dad, I'm gray.'

”

Mitchell recalls the memory of coming out to Jay – an experience that took quite a few tries.

Season 1, Episode 13: "Fifteen Percent"
"35+ 'Modern Family' Quotes To Make You Feel Like A Tucker-Pritchett-Dunphy", scarymommy.com, January 22, 2021

You're missing out on life, Mitchell. Take off your shackles and show people who you really are.

”

Cam encourages Mitchell to be his true self in front of the world.

Season 10, Episode 6: "On the Same Paige"
"100 Best Quotes from *Modern Family*", sarahscoop.com, August 22, 2022

“

I was painting sunflowers outside, and I got stung by a bee. I took it as a compliment.

”

Mitchell, in his Van Gogh era while taking a break from employment.

Season 7, Episode 1: "Summer Lovin'"
"*Modern Family*: One Quote From Each Main Character That Goes Against Their Personality", screenrant.com, October 1, 2021

I won cutest baby at the 1974 Jasper County Fair. People at the time said I could go Gerber.

Cam, on his childhood fame.

Season 3, Episode 7: "Treehouse"
"18 Times *Modern Family*'s Cam Cracked You Up", popsugar.com, May 19, 2016

We have been renting the upstairs unit to some frat boys from Cam's old college. They're here for some big game and to try to get on *The Price is Right*. Unfortunately for me, it's brought out Cam's bromosexual side.

Mitchell tires of the renters living in the apartment upstairs.

Season 7, Episode 4: "She Crazy"
modernfamily.fandom.com

Is this kindergarten or *The Hunger Games*?

”

Cam questions the safety of Lily's school.

Season 4, Episode 2: "Schooled"
modernfamily.fandom.com

So, a karaoke bar, huh? You know, it's a little offensive that you think singing a pop song is gonna solve my problems. How gay do you think I am?

”

Mitchell questions how his dad sees him – ironically, Jay hit the nail on the head, and singing Madonna at a karaoke bar is exactly what helps Mitchell feel better.

Season 7, Episode 17: "Express Yourself"
modernfamily.fandom.com

"

Why not just live your limited days with leaving nothing unsaid. Tell the people who matter the most how you feel.

"

Cam, reminding the family to express their true feelings to each other.

Season 10, Episode 17: "The Wild"
"*Modern Family*: 13 Best Inspiring Quotes About Relationships", screenrant.com, November 16, 2021

Fizbo Is Real!

Cameron's Fizbo persona wasn't invented by the show's writers.

Eric Stonestreet actually performed as Fizbo the Clown at birthday parties when he was a kid.

His father came up with the name, and his grandmother made the costumes.

“

Oh, yeah. They serve your rural gays, your closeted gays, your city newbies looking to get their gay sea-legs, kind of like an out-of-town tryout before they hit Broadway.

”

Mitchell, on small-town gay bars and those who frequent them.

Season 10, Episode 8: "Kids These Days"
"21 Quotes We Love From *Modern Family*'s Mitchell Pritchett!", parade.com, March 6, 2021

That's a lot of complaining for somebody who asked for thirds of our tandoori turkey last year.

”

Cam reminds Claire of how much she actually enjoyed their unconventional Thanksgiving.

Season 2, Episode 6: "Halloween"
"17 Comebacks From Cameron Tucker From 'Modern Family' That Made Me Go 'SLAYYY'", buzzfeed.com, June 8, 2022

CHAPTER five

That's Offensive

Whether it's Haley's effortless burns, Gloria's fiery roasts, or Cam delivering drama with a side of sass, no moment is safe from a perfectly timed zinger.

From sassy retorts to hilariously blunt truths, these comebacks weren't just funny – they were iconic. Because in this household, humour isn't just a defence mechanism… it's a way of life.

That is so offensive. A lisp doesn't make you gay. Being gay makes you lisp.

Gloria clears up how offensive people can be…

Season 8, Episode 4: "Weathering Heights"
imdb.com

There's a fish in nature that swims around with its babies in its mouth. That fish would look at Mitchell's relationship with his mother and say, 'That's messed up.'

99

Cam, on Mitchell's unusual relationship with his mother.

Season 1, Episode 4: "The Incident"
"35+ 'Modern Family' Quotes To Make You Feel Like A Tucker-Pritchett-Dunphy", scarymommy.com, January 22, 2021

Yeah, well, my mother canceled in a voicemail and told me she had a boyfriend in a newsletter, so join the team.

Mitchell, after Alex exclaims: "My mom tells me it's 'Xmas' in a text?"

Season 3, Episode 10: "Express Christmas"
modernfamily.fandom.com

Sweeping the Awards Scene

Modern Family won a total of 22 Primetime Emmy Awards and 6 Writers Guild of America Awards, proving that snarky one-liners and heartwarming family moments can be a winning combination.

You want to hear the guest list for the night? So far it's anger, betrayal, terror, and sadness. Congratulations, Mitchell, you packed the house!

”

Cam despairs when Mitchell forgets to mail the invitations for an event he is hosting.

Season 2, Episode 16: "Regrets Only"
"35+ 'Modern Family' Quotes To Make You Feel Like A Tucker-Pritchett-Dunphy", scarymommy.com, January 22, 2021

Well, you tricked me into coming here, you made me gay, now I have a boyfriend. All these lies just to win a trophy. I respect that.

”

Jay credits Cam for his efforts to win a bowling competition.

Season 6, Episode 20: "Knock 'Em Down"
transcripts.foreverdreaming.org

Honey, you're not unlikeable… You just seem unlikeable.

”

Phil, gently breaking to Claire that people don't like her when she runs for City Council (and ultimately loses, although she does get the STOP sign she petitioned for).

Season 3, Episode 15: "Aunt Mommy"
modernfamily.fandom.com

It's where the planet geek passes through the nerdy way.

”

Cam jokes about Mitchell's tradition of going stargazing with his dad.

Season 1, Episode 18: "Starry Night"
"17 Comebacks From Cameron Tucker From 'Modern Family' That Made Me Go 'SLAYYY'", buzzfeed.com, June 8, 2022

You're sneakier than I am... You have no moral compass.

”

Manny, to Luke, asking for help sneaking into a Bar Mitzvah. Luke responds (seriously): "Thanks for all the compliments."

Season 4, Episode 8: "Mistery Date"
"*Modern Family*: 10 Iconic Quotes That Perfectly Sum Up Luke & Manny's Relationship", screenrant.com, September 29, 2022

He's my husband's uncle. Oh, you look confused? A husband is somebody who loves you that you don't have to pay.

”

Cam, to his rival, during a bowling competition – Jay (his husband's father, not uncle) is pretending to be gay… all to win a trophy.

Season 6, Episode 20: "Knock 'Em Down"
transcripts.foreverdreaming.org

The last time Haley informed me of her plans, she said, 'Ha ha, I'm going to Cabo and you're not.'

Alex, to Andy, whose responding laugh reveals his romantic feelings for Haley.

Season 6, Episode 19: "Grill, Interrupted"
transcripts.foreverdreaming.org

Here's the deal. Girls don't go for all that romantic stuff. They go for power and success, and since you don't have either one of those things… you're gonna be the funny guy.

Jay gives Manny some fatherly advice on how to play on his strengths.

Season 1, Episode 9: "Fizbo"
"25 Hilarious *Modern Family* Quotes to Live By", readersdigest.ca

You had your summer of the red afro, and I dated the whitest Puerto Rican on Earth.

”

Claire, to Mitchell, on their rebellious phase as teenagers.

Season 6, Episode 19: "Grill, Interrupted"
yarn.co

A Show That Went the Distance

Modern Family ran for 11 seasons and 250 episodes, making it ABC's longest-running comedy.

It officially ended in April 2020, leaving behind a legacy of sarcasm, sass and unforgettable comebacks.

You're really judging me right now when you look like a hooker at Comic-Con?

Alex, to Claire, when she judges her choice in romantic partners.

Season 7, Episode 7: "Phil's Sexy, Sexy House"
"100 Best Quotes from *Modern Family*", sarahscoop.com, August 22, 2022

Maybe spend a little less time with your nose in that psych book and a little more time being sexy.

”

Phil, to Luke, when Luke's crush was using him to get to Phil. On a seemingly (un)related note, Luke's crush had major realtor/magician/daddy issues.

Season 10, Episode 6: "On the Same Paige"
"100 Best Quotes from *Modern Family*", sarahscoop.com, August 22, 2022

In *Legally Blonde*, Elle won her case because she was true to herself and dressed cute.

Haley reminds her parents of how to win against the law, after getting arrested for assaulting a police officer at college (she fell on top of him accidentally). Phil responds with: "Haley this is real life, not an excellent movie."

Season 4, Episode 7: "Arrested"
"100 Best Quotes from *Modern Family*", sarahscoop.com, August 22, 2022

Cry me a river…
Sorry, should I call you
a wahmbulance?

”

Lily's first signs of sass – influenced by Claire… It only gets more sarcastic from here.

Season 4, Episode 13: "Fulgencio"
"*Modern Family*: Lily's 10 Sassiest Quotes", screenrant.com, June 6, 2019

Sexy people go crazy too, you know. Read a *People* magazine.

”

Haley reminds the world that you can be hot and a little insane at the same time.

Season 2, Episode 6: "Halloween"
"*Modern Family*: Best Haley Dunphy Quotes", screenrant.com, May 9, 2019

Oh, here we go. Because in Colombia, we trip over goats, and we kill people in the street. Do you know how offensive that is?

”

Gloria reminds Jay to stop stereotyping Latin America… or at least, Colombia.

Season 2, Episode 5: "Unplugged"
"20 Unapologetic Quotes By *Modern Family*'s Gloria That Make Her TV's Feistiest Character", July 5, 2016, scoopwhoop.com

We never needed fake IDs on the farm. We figured if a 16-year-old could drive a tractor, he could drink a beer. Not at the same time, of course. It's Missouri, not Texas.

”

Cam clears up any misconceptions of Missouri being similar to Texas.

Season 3, Episode 5: "Hit and Run"
"17 Comebacks From Cameron Tucker From 'Modern Family' That Made Me Go 'SLAYYY'", buzzfeed.com, June 8, 2022

When you mess with Phil Dunphy, the claws come out.

Phil reminds us that he's not one to mess with.

Season 2, Episode 17: "Two Monkeys and a Panda"
modernfamily.fandom.com

Belle's a princess. She faced the beast. She stood up to the townspeople. What have you done?

”

Lily, to Clare, who responds, "I got us into that tiny, little parking spot."

Season 5, Episode 17: "Other People's Children"
"*Modern Family*: Lily's 10 Sassiest Quotes", screenrant.com, June 6, 2019

You're too funny. I'm gonna share that one with my next husband when we're spending your money.

99

Gloria, to Jay, countering his jokes with her own.

Season 1, Episode 2: "The Bicycle Thief"
"20 Unapologetic Quotes By *Modern Family's* Gloria That Make Her TV's Feistiest Character", July 5, 2016, scoopwhoop.com

CHAPTER six

When Life Gives You Lemonade

In the *Modern Family* universe, wisdom comes in many forms – sometimes heartfelt, sometimes hilariously misguided.

Whether it's Phil's offbeat optimism, Jay's tough love or Gloria's fiery determination, the family proves that life's chaos is best handled with laughter, resilience and maybe a perfectly timed *Dunphyism* from the famous *Phil's-osophy*.

Because when life gets confusing, why not confuse it right back?

The most amazing things that can happen to a human being will happen if you just lower your expectations.

”

Phil shares some of the iconic dad wisdom in his book *Phil's-osophy.*

Season 4, Episode 2: "Schooled"
"11 of the Funniest Real Estate Quotes (and Advice) from *Modern Family's* Phil Dunphy", labcoatagents.com, July 20, 2020

We do strange things for the people we love... There may be bumps along the way, but we never stop wanting the best for them.

Claire, on the things we do for the ones we love.

Season 1, Episode 6: "Run for Your Wife"
"The 10 Best 'Modern Family' Quotes, Ranked", collider.com, February 23, 2024

Everybody's desperately afraid, to be different, you know, in any way. And then, suddenly, almost overnight, everybody wants to be different. And that is where we win.

”

Mitchell, to Manny, on being proud to be unique.

Season 1, Episode 18: "Starry Night"
"The 10 Best 'Modern Family' Quotes, Ranked", collider.com, February 23, 2024

I'm not here to spit in your face; I'm here to blow at your back… It's supposed to sound better in Spanish.

Jay, repeating a phrase that Gloria taught him – admittedly, it sounds much more poetic in Spanish: *Voy a ser la brisa en tu espalda, no quien te escupa en la frente.*

Season 1, Episode 1: "Pilot"
modernfamily.fandom.com

We like to think we are so smart, and we have all the answers. And we want to pass all that on to our children, but if you scratch beneath the surface you don't have to dig very deep to find the kid you were. Which is kind of crazy that now we're raising kids of our own. I guess that's the real circle of life. Your parents faked their way through it. You fake your way through it. And you just hope you didn't raise a serial killer.

”

Phil, on doing his best to raise his kids well while feeling like one himself.

Season 2, Episode 10: "Dance Dance Revelation"
"*Modern Family*: 13 Best Inspiring Quotes About Relationships", screenrant.com, November 16, 2021

Breaking the Fourth Wall

Modern Family was originally called *My American Family* and the show's original premise was completely different.

Co-creator Christopher Lloyd originally envisioned Modern Family as a documentary filmed by a Dutch filmmaker who had lived with Jay's family as an exchange student. This concept was eventually dropped, but the mockumentary style remained.

This style of filming allowed the actors to consistently break the fourth wall.

When life gives you lemonade, make lemons. Life will be all like, 'Whaaat?!'

Phil gives us one of his most iconic pieces of advice.

Season 4, Episode 2: "Schooled"
"25 Hilarious *Modern Family* Quotes to Live By", readersdigest.ca

Back in '68, when I was sweeping up hair in that barbershop, I had this mental picture of the family that, if I was lucky enough, I would end up with. Perfect wife, perfect kids… Well, guess what? I didn't get any of that. I wound up with this sorry bunch. And I'm thankful for that every day. Well, most days.

”

Jay reminisces about the life he dreamed, and the dream he lives now.

Season 1, Episode 24: "Family Portrait"
modernfamily.fandom.com

Success is 1% inspiration, 98% perspiration, and 2% attention to detail.

”

Phil shares more of this inspiring wisdom in *Phil's-osophy.*

Season 4, Episode 2: "Schooled"
"The 10 Best 'Modern Family' Quotes, Ranked", collider.com, February 23, 2024

There are dreamers and there are realists in this world. You think the dreamers would find the dreamers and the realists would find the realists, but more often than not, the opposite is true. You see, the dreamers need the realists to keep them from soaring too close to the sun. And the realists, well, without the dreamers, they might never get off the ground.

Cam reminds us of how people's differences are what bring them together.

Season 3, Episode 9: "Punkin Chunkin"
"*Modern Family*: 13 Best Inspiring Quotes About Relationships", screenrant.com, November 16, 2021

Take a lesson from parakeets. If you ever feel lonely, just eat in front of a mirror.

”

Haley reads **Phil's** dad advice in *Phil's-osophy*, as she settles into college.

Season 4, Episode 2: "Schooled"
"100 Best Quotes from *Modern Family*", sarahscoop.com, August 22, 2022

People can surprise you. You can get used to thinking of them one way... Then they do something that shows you there's all this depth and dimension that you never knew existed.

”

Mitchell remembers that people can be more versatile than they seem.

Season 2, Episode 18: "Boys' Night"
"*Modern Family*: 13 Best Inspiring Quotes About Relationships", screenrant.com, November 16, 2021

A Show Built on Improvization

The cast was often encouraged to improvize, and some of the best moments – including many of Cam's over-the-top reactions and young Lily's ad-libs – were completely unscripted.

Jesse Tyler Ferguson (Mitchell Pritchett) told *Interview* magazine: "You can't stop Lily from ad libbing. That's like stopping a moving train. It's my job to keep up with what she was throwing at me… It was about 30% improv, and that was Lily throwing the ball in my court to see if I could volley."

"Jesse Tyler Ferguson: The Bemused Exasperation Expert", *Interview* magazine, October 16, 2012

Every time anyone accomplishes anything, [they] achieve it with the help of a thousand silent heroes.

”

Alex credits her family for always supporting her in the background.

Season 6, Episode 21: "Integrity"
"*Modern Family*: 13 Best Inspiring Quotes About Relationships", screenrant.com, November 16, 2021

It's gonna be tough to say goodbye… it always is. Nobody loves change. But part of life is learning to let things go.

”

Phil shares some fatherly advice about saying goodbye.

Season 2, Episode 1: "The Old Wagon"
"*Modern Family*: 13 Best Inspiring Quotes About Relationships", screenrant.com, November 16, 2021

It's scary to let people see the real you. Even when those people are your own family. But aren't they the ones we should be least worried about? The ones who will love us without judging? Who will forgive our faults and celebrate our imperfections? Maybe even encourage us to let our true selves shine through?

”

Manny remembers that family are the people you can be your true self around.

Season 5, Episode 21: "Sleeper"
modernfamily.fandom.com

Those fears you never get past. So sometimes all you have to do is take a deep breath, hold them close and hope for the best.

”

Phil isn't afraid to admit his fears as an adult and a father.

Season 1, Episode 16: "Fears"
"*Modern Family*: 13 Best Inspiring Quotes About Relationships", screenrant.com, November 16, 2021

You're obviously going to get into one of those snooty schools, and sometimes you're gonna come in second. Or fourth. Or maybe even tenth. But you're gonna dust yourself off, maybe put on some lipstick for once, and keep going.

”

Haley Dunphy

Season 6, Episode 18: "Spring Break"
"*Modern Family*: Best Haley Dunphy Quotes", screenrant.com, May 9, 2019

Think inside the box. That's right, I said inside. Because while everyone is chasing each other outside, what is the box? Empty.

”

Phil finds a way to be different with some more unusual dad wisdom.

Season 4, Episode 5: "Open House of Horrors"
"11 of the Funniest Real Estate Quotes (and Advice) from *Modern Family*'s Phil Dunphy", labcoatagents.com, July 20, 2020

“

Keep your head up, don’t look back. Being right is mostly confidence.

”

Cam, to Mitchell, after he gives a passionate speech to their friends.

Season 6, Episode 22: "Patriot Games"
transcripts.foreverdreaming.org

There are all kinds of milestones in life. The kind you expect to live through… first kiss, birthdays, graduations… And then there's the kind you never dream you'd get to live through again. And that's the best kind of all.

”

Jay, on growing older and feeling grateful for life's experiences.

Season 4, Episode 12: "Party Crasher"
"6 'Modern Family' Quotes That Apply To Your Swim Family", *Swimming World* magazine, May 26, 2016

Family is family. Whether it's the one you start out with, the one you end up with, or the family you gain along the way.

Gloria, on the family she married into that became her own.

Season 3, Episode 10: "Express Christmas"
"*Modern Family*: 13 Best Inspiring Quotes About Relationships", screenrant.com, November 16, 2021

“

Dance until your feet hurt, sing until your lungs hurt, act until you’re William Hurt.

”

Phil’s inspiring *Phil’s-osophies* are never-ending… and they never get old.

Season 4, Episode 2: “Schooled”
"*Modern Family*: The 8 Weirdest Quotes From The Show", cbr.com, May 31, 2022

The hero in my family is my family, because of who we are together.

”

Manny shares his heartfelt thoughts on heroes for a school paper – he gets a C, because he was supposed to choose just one hero.

Season 4, Episode 22: "My Hero"
"*Modern Family*: 13 Best Inspiring Quotes About Relationships", screenrant.com, November 16, 2021

Life is full of change – some big, some small. I learned a long time ago you can fight it, or you can try to make the best of it. And that's all a lot easier if you've got people who love you, helping you face whatever life throws at you.

”

Jay shares some of his wisdom in the very last episode of the show.

Season 11, Episode 18: Finale: Part 2
"*Modern Family*: 13 Best Inspiring Quotes About Relationships", screenrant.com, November 16, 2021